HOW TO PLAY

BADMINTON

PAT DAVIS

TREASURE PRESS

Contents

796.34

First published in Great Britain in 1979 by
The Hamlyn Publishing Group Limited

This edition published in 1989 by
Treasure Press
Michelin House
81 Fulham Road
London
SW3 6RB

ISBN 1 85051 409 7

Printed in Yugoslavia

Meet The Coach!

There are no two ways about it! Personal coaching is much better that book coaching. But it's much, much more expensive too— about 100 times more. So let's make the best of this tutor, which is always unquestioningly at your service.

You, the reader, are one or other of that charming couple, Sam and Samantha; not the impersonal, disembodied 'the player', nor the coldly austere 'one', nor the oddly bisexual 'he/she'. The author is the coach (and in fact he is used to coaching complete beginners – as well as top players – despite being a Badminton Association of England National Coach).

Years of coaching have taught me that, with a little initial prompting, my students learn more by intelligent observation of a demonstration than they do by just listening to my exposition. Television makes more impact than radio. Similarly, in this book (whenever possible) action speaks louder than words. So in each photo thoughtfully observe the position of: the player on court; the feet and legs; the body; the arm and wrist; the racket; the shuttle; and where the player is looking.

But don't, for heaven's sake, get the idea that the words are just there to fill the pages. They speak volumes if you read them equally thoughtfully. One final point – this book has been written with right-handed players in mind; left-handers should simply reverse all the directions.

Thinking Point : To learn, carefully watch the expert as well as listen to him.

Pat Davis

Chapter One
Why Badminton?

There are at least half a dozen good reasons! Played indoors, mainly in winter, it provides exercise and fun despite the snow, fog, rain and darkness of winter. Wielding a $3\frac{1}{2}$ ounce racket and hitting a $\frac{1}{4}$-ounce shuttle provide no problems for anyone. It is a game at which any person with even a modicum of ball sense can soon be having rallies. And clubs have a flourishing social side.

It is played in almost every town and village throughout the length and breadth of this country. More evening classes are run to teach badminton than to teach any other game. And when your first faltering steps become eager strides, you find badminton is so well organised that the excitement of competitive league and tournament play is available everywhere.

If you like to be in the swim, know that 'Badminton has Background'. It is played in some 60 foreign countries with keen

Indonesia's Chandra (left) and Christian (right), one of the world's greatest doubles pairs, show the agility, speed and power essential in top-flight badminton.

international rivalry between nations such as world champions China (Thomas Cup holders – for men and also Uber Cup holders – for women), Malaysia and Japan and the Western countries such as England, Denmark, Sweden, Holland and Canada. The All-England Championships, held at Wembley Pool every March, is the mecca of badminton to which leading players travel from all over the world. Moreover, badminton has become Open! This means more frequent appearances of world-class players, big-money sponsorship and more frequent television spots.

Seize these chances to see badminton at its best: a game of swift and graceful movement, of power play contrastingly highlighted by a delicacy of touch, of wrong-footing deception, of incredible retrieving and lightning interception, and of varied chess-like tactics of singles, doubles and mixed doubles – each an absorbing and different game in its own right.

So jump on the band-wagon now for fitness, friends and fun. The cost? Initial equipment can be quite cheap and thereafter badminton costs comparatively little when you consider the health and enjoyment it generates compared to activities such as smoking or drinking. And does you much more good, Sam!

No need for qualms about starting. If you've played at school – and today nearly every school plays badminton – the ever-growing legions of clubs will be glad to have you as a member. Find the local club secretary's address from your local sports shop, public library or newspaper. Or failing that, drop a line to the Badminton Association of England, Bradwell Road, Loughton Lodge, Milton Keynes MK8 9LA.

If you haven't played before, clubs will naturally not be quite so eager. Let's face it, even the pleasantest or prettiest 'bunny' spoils an experienced 'four'. Never worry! Use this book intelligently and you'll soon reach an acceptable club standard.

So, go to it. There's a lifetime of pleasurable exercise ahead of you in badminton!

Chapter Two
How To Play And Practise

Playing

If you win the spin of the racket ('rough' or 'smooth' – ascertained by touch of the coloured trebbing at the bottom of the racket), you can elect either to serve or choose ends. Your opponents take up your rejected option.

If you decide to serve (in doubles) one of you serves from the right hand court, underhand, to the service court diagonally opposite. The receiver returns the shuttle anywhere into your court. Thereafter it is hit by one of each pair in turn until one side 'faults'. (*Partners* do not have to play the shuttle strictly in turn).

It is a 'fault' if you fail to return the shuttle over the net into court or break certain specific rules which will be explained later. A fault by the serving (or 'in') side results in the loss of his service by the player serving; service then passes (except after the initial rally of each game) to his partner. A fault by the receiving (or 'out' side) results in a point gained by the 'in' side. In that event, the server continues serving and changes sides with his partner so as not to serve to the same receiver twice in succession. Thus a player continues serving, scoring a point and changing over as long as his side wins the rallies. However, when the 'in' side have faulted twice and thus lost both serves, the serve passes to the opponent in the righthand court. They in turn continue as above . . . and so on.

In singles, sides are similarly changed when a point is scored. Remember that when your score is an even number you serve from the right service court; when it is odd, from the left.

Thinking Point : Know the rules!

Scoring

Remember, a point is scored only when a rally is won by the serving side. (In singles, when the receiver wins a rally a point is not scored, but instead the receiver wins the right to serve). The score is called always with the server's score first, say, 1–0 (one-love), 2–0, 3–0, then, when serve passes to the opponent, the score becomes 0–3, 1–3, 2–3, 3–3 (three-all), etc. In addition, in doubles when the second player starts to serve, add 'second server' thus '2–3, second server', '3–3, second server', '4–3, second server'. Then perhaps, after a fault by the in side, '3–4', and after a fault by the new 'in' side, '3–4, second server'. The score continues thus until one pair scores 15 points. To avoid argument always call the score aloud, know which half-court you should be in to serve or to receive, and whether it is first server, or second server.

There is one slight complication if the scores become 13-all or

14-all. In both cases, the pair which first reach 13 or 14 have the option of playing straight through normally to 15 or of 'setting'. This means the score reverts to love all and, at 13 all, playing up to a further 5 points, i.e. 18, or, at 14 all a further 3 points to 17. Refusal to 'set' at 13 all does not preclude setting at 14 all.

Ladies' singles, even in this era of Women's Lib, is to 11 up, not 15 up. Setting is at 9 all and 10 all for a further 3 points and 2 points respectively.

At the end of the first game, the pairs change ends. The winning pair start the serving. If they lose the second game, a third deciding game is played. In this the pairs again change sides at 8 (6 in ladies' singles).

How To Practise

Nobody likes a loser – or losing! Flip through the whole book first if you like, then come back. Read through, not a chapter ('overhead strokes') at a time but a single, short section ('the smash'). Read that attentively until it is 'grooved' in. When you're sure, shadow a stroke thoughtfully on an imaginary court with an imaginary shuttle. *Correct* mental and shadowing stroke-play can improve actual play. Next, book a regular court at your local Sports Centre or go down early to grab a vacant club court. To begin with, discipline yourself to two-thirds practice, one-third actual play.

Thinking Point : Only perfect practice makes perfect.

Always check how near you come to the desired end-product; smash – fast and steep, to target; low serve – tape-skimming and dropping into court; clears high and good length. Start simply: shuttle hit *to* you, one stroke at a time. Don't try to run before you can walk by rallying yet. Simplify further still if success eludes

Diagram 1 : Measurements and nomenclature of a badminton court.

2ft 6in 0.76	13ft 0in 3.96m	6ft 6in 1.98m Side Line	6ft 6in 1.98m for Doubles	13ft 0in 3.96m	2ft 6in 0.76

Left Service Court · Side Line : for Singles · Right Service Court

Centre Line · Centre Line

Right Service Court · Side Line : for Singles · Left Service Court

also Long Service Line for Singles · Back Boundary Line; · Long Service Line for Doubles · Short Service Line · Short Service Line · Long Service Line for Doubles · also Long Service Line for Singles · Back Boundary Line;

20ft 0in 6.10m

Side Line · for Doubles
44ft 0in
13.40m

18in 0.46
17ft 0in 5.18m
18in 0.46

you; if you can't make contact in, say, the clear, cut out the difficulty of the back-swing and *start* with racket dropped down over your shoulder. Finally, keep count and note down success rate; e.g. '6 out of 10 smashes over the net but not steep enough'. Make some of your practice competitive – all of it enjoyable.

At The Club On club nights there's nothing to stop you occasionally using your quarter of an hour for straight practice, rather than just another game from which little is learnt. Later, even if you play a game you can still practise a stroke (keep every serve low; smash anything lifted into the body) or a game tactic (high serve to the lady; return of low serve to the net). It requires dedication.

Build up gradually in this way until you are ready for competitive play – the fire in which your skills are fine-tempered. After each game – win or lose – hold an intelligently analytical inquiry (not a back-biting post-mortem) into success and failure alike.

Court Courtesies

Look your best – behave your best! It is all too easy to breach simple badminton etiquette if unaware of it. So, remember:

If games are made up by a Committee member, don't grumble if you are 'hutched' with other 'bunnies'. If you make up your own games don't ask the club's 'tiger'; it's no game for him – and it's no game for you! Ask someone who is just 4–5 points better.

Give, fairly and clearly, line decisions for *your* side of the net only; never for the other – even if you are long-sighted! If only part of the shuttle is on the line, it is still in. Give the benefit of slight doubts to your opponent though never be too quixotic. Real doubts, ask for a 'let' replay.

If you get even the most delicate of touches of the shuttle before your partner hits it, if the shuttle just brushes your hair or clothing, or if you touch the net in any way, it is up to *you* to call 'fault' appropriately.

Shuttles that you hit into your side of the net or that have dropped onto the floor on your side are your responsibility. Pick them up and *hand* them to your partner, or throw or hit them accurately to your opponent(s). Never scrape them under the net.

Encourage your partner: don't growl and grunt – or even raise beseeching eyes to Heaven!

Never make excuses in defeat or be cocky in victory.

Never walk on or even behind another court during a rally. Wait until it ends, then walk *briskly* across at the back.

One player should always keep the score: if you are asked, call it clearly at the end of each rally.

If sitting beside a court, don't talk distractingly loudly.

Take your fair share of club chores.

Positively no 'Nasty' dissent or racket-throwing tantrums. Be competitive but absolutely fair.

Thinking Point: Hall marks of a badminton player: Courtesy! Fairness! Sportsmanship!

Chapter Three
Fitness

In the game of badminton, power of stroke, fleetness of foot and stamina are essential foundations. Just a little less TV lounging and you (indeed everyone) could be really fit. This is a home DIY job – no need for elaborate equipment, just a little will-power.

Clockwise from top: the wrist-strengthener; the step-up; leg raise to strengthen the abdomen; the press-up.

Basic Fitness
Jog for basic fitness; build up gradually.

Progress to jog (85 yards) then sprint (15 yards) and so on.

Agility
Skip with rope; run between skittles set close together.

Suppleness
Do 'Popmobility' exercises to the latest hit tunes. (Write to Robinson's Barley Water for details). Fun and fitness together!

Power
Arm-strength : Press-ups (ladies from a kneeling position).

Wrist-strength : 1 securely tie a brick with a five foot length of string to half a broom handle. With arms outstretched, roll the brick up to the stick; *roll* it down again – don't just let it run down. *2* when you carry a heavy shopping basket constantly raise and lower it solely by cocking and uncocking the wrist.

Abdomen
Lie flat on the floor; raise legs slowly to 45°; lower even more slowly to six inches from floor. Hold!

Speed
Legs : Step-ups. Simply step up and down onto a chair or bench 18 inches high as fast as you can for 90 or 120 seconds *or* skip jump over a nine-inch bench; *or*, upright, feet together, spring up and touch the wall as high as you can.

Shuttle-runs : Sprint ten yards forwards and back making five 'double' journeys of 20 yards each. The return run can be made actually running backwards. Repeat three times allowing one minute rest intervals.

Five-yard dashes : backwards as well as forwards.

Remember badminton is largely starting, stopping, twisting, bending and turning! For fitness . . . it's worth the effort!

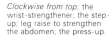

Chapter Four
Equipment

Good equipment doesn't make a player, but it certainly helps. So
buy wisely – if a little extravagantly.

Rackets

There are four main types of racket:

1 All-metal (rather heavy but durable);
2 Steel-shafted but with a T-piece and a light aluminium head;
3 One piece of carbon or graphite and fibre glass (lighter and
  whippier);
4 One piece graphite and boron or ceramic (durable and very light).

Choose a well-known make (Carlton, Browning, Slazenger, Pro
Kennex, RSL, Yonex, etc). Choose one that feels right, light and
neither head nor handle heavy. Pick it up; get the feel of it; play
imaginary strokes. (Look out for those lights, Sam!)

Whichever you choose, see it has these qualities:

1 A weight of four ounces or less;
2 A leather perforated grip which fits comfortably into your hand;
3 A shaft with whip (Flex it gently; it's not an iron bar);
4 Tight stringing with thin, clear, natural gut. This should yield
only very slightly to thumb pressure and should give a high 'ping'
when flicked with a finger-nail.

A racket is expensive so look after it!

Never (even in agonies of self-abjuration) throw it about.

Never shovel shuttles along the floor with it.

Never use it when strings are broken.

Keep strings from heat or damp.

Shuttles

These are generally supplied by the club but to know their
qualities is to appreciate them more: 16 matched feathers from two
geese; 80 grains of gossamer-fragile strength leaving the racket at
up to 100 mph.

Feathered shuttles are still the best for flight, turnover and
touch, but they tend to be rather high on cost and low on life
expectancy. Synthetic nylon shuttles (RSL Competition and
Carlton Tournament are examples) are fine for beginners and club
players; and thanks to intensive research they are steadily improving. Generally less expensive and often rather more durable than
feathered shuttles, some have cork bases and some are coloured
yellow for better sighting.

A shuttle is of a correct speed if, when hit by a player of average
strength from above one back line in an upward (45) trajectory,
it lands within nine inches of the doubles back service line.
Obviously it is important to know if your shuttle is fast or slow,
so don't hesitate to test it before and even during a game.

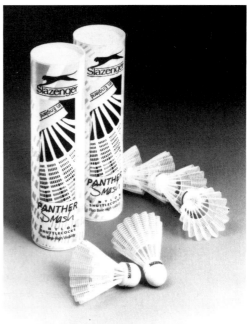

Remember, speeds change when use alters the feathers' spread or hall temperatures rise or fall. The speed of shuttles varies and this is indicated by the differing weights or colours printed on the tubes. For instance, at a temperature of 50° Fahrenheit (10° Centigrade) a feathered shuttle of 75–77 grains or a green plastic shuttle would be used in a small village hall with one court, a feathered shuttle of 78–79 grains or a blue shuttle would be used in a school gym, a feathered shuttle of 80–81 grains or a red shuttle would be used in a hall with two or three courts, and a feathered shuttle of 82–84 grains or a red shuttle would be used in a lofty sports hall with four or more courts. Remember, the hotter the hall, the faster and farther a shuttle flies.

Photograph: Courtesy of Carlton and Slazenger.

Because they are scarce and expensive, treat feathered shuttles with particular care:

1 Never – either in pique or desperation – hit a shuttle on the half-volley as it hits the floor.

2 Never bang a tube of shuttles or pull a shuttle out the wrong way, feathers first.

3 Store in a cool, slightly moist place (nylon shuttles improve with gentle warmth); don't crush them.

4 Always smooth ruffled barbs with fingers not racket strings.

Thinking Point: Save Our Shuttles; Save your pocket.

Clothing

This is virtually the same as for tennis and squash. Names to conjure with are Bukta, Litesome and Slazenger. 'Wear white' is still the cry, but colour stripes and panels are now acceptable both for men and women.

Pedro Blach and Gillian Gilks
show the standards to aim at
in dress. Clothing containing
a high degree of cotton or
wool is the most comfortable
as it absorbs perspiration
best.

A bewildering choice is yours, but whatever you choose make
sure that it is: brief and loose-fitting to give ease of full arm and
leg movement; of absorbent material to cope with perspiration.
And finally, wear a tracksuit, which will keep you warm and will
also help prevent pulled muscles.

Shoes

Well-chosen, these can add useful mph to your speed about court.
See that they are light and flexible, fit snugly, lace up to the
instep, and have stout toe-caps, well-ridged durable soles, ventila-
tion holes, and sponge rubber inners. (For tacky floors, or portable
Hova courts, it is as well to have a smoother sole to give just a
little slide.)

And please, Sam, a bottle of . . . Meltonian whiting. Grey shoes
betoken the apprentice – not the craftsman. So keep 'em clean!
Finally, wear woollen socks; they help prevent blisters.

Hold-all

Besides clothing and rackets, keep in a side pocket, safety pins,
absorbent wristlets, a resin pad, racket handle gauze, spectacle
de-mister and headband, salt tablets, plasters, talc, glucose ener-
gising drink, spare laces . . . oh, and a copy of the laws for peaceful
settlement of any arguments. Take them court-side as a security
measure for play must be continuous.

Thinking Point : Look the part : Feel the part : Play the part.

Chapter Five
Basic Essentials

Just think for yourself for a moment which parts of your body are going to play really vital roles in your game. Obviously eye, hand, arm and wrist, legs and feet. (Let's not forget either the invisible vital cardio-vascular attributes of heart and lungs.)

Grip
Heaven knows you two have been very patient so let's give you the first feel of that delicate, whippy racket you're longing to use. There are three possible grips.

Basic which can be used for all strokes.

Frying-pan which is solely for dab shots at or near the net.

Backhand which is for those shots on the left side of the body.

Let's take each in turn, then see how easily we can switch from one to the other.

Basic Grip 'Grip it right; hit it right!' is a good maxim. For the basic grip, Sam, hold the racket by the head and, with the edge at right angles to the ground, proffer the handle to Samantha. Now . . . simply shake hands, Samantha.

Don't grip it like a vice – or a vicar. But do be sure the racket is firmly held at impact. Check and check again that:

1 the V between thumb and fore-finger points roughly down the top bevel in line with the frame: arm, hand and racket are now one long lever, aren't they?

2 your index finger is spaced a little apart from the other three which are curling together round the butt end of the handle; this gives you a finger (not palm) grip. Essential for real feel and touch.

3 You've paid for all the racket, Samantha, so hold it lower down with only the butt-end just protruding. That's for reach and power.

Fine! Hold the racket frame-on to the net, with the firm delicacy of an artist, a surgeon, a violinist. After all a five ounce (or less) racket does not need a Titan's club-swinging crushing grip, Sam. To hit with the face of the racket turn your wrist, *not* the racket in your hand. The latter gives you the frying-pan grip.

Frying-pan Grip This, with the racket-face held square to the net, is ideal for downward dabbing of net shots and serves. At the back of the court it is anathema for it leads to those debilitating and crippling ailments of bent arm and stiff wrist. Vital power and steepness are lost.

Backhand Grip Hold the racket in the basic grip, then turn the racket some 30° to the right. Now place the flat of the thumb directly *up* the flat back bevel of the handle. Turn the wrist to the left to open the racket-face again. Do you feel how this gives you a little more leverage and control? Welcome qualities in a frail back-hand. Now practise switching from one grip to the other in a split

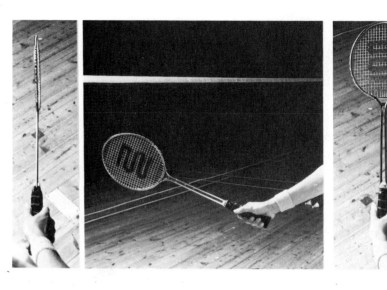

second simply by loosening the grip and rolling the racket in the fingers. Forehand – backhand – frying-pan – backhand . . . !

Wrist

This is the lynch-pin of all strokes except the low serve and net-shots. It bears invaluable gifts: extra, effortless 'zip' for power shots; angle; elevation; deception. In tennis, the impact of a fast-moving two ounce ball on a heavy 15 ounce racket needs a locked wrist. Not so with a featherweight shuttle! So use and enjoy that wrist to the full. Snap it crisply backwards and forwards.

Observe it for a moment. See how, with the racket vertical and frame to the net, not only can you turn the wrist left and right to give direction but also backwards and forwards to give elevation as well as zip. Try it. Loosen that wrist! Use this wonderful universal joint crisply, but not in an over-eager snatch which can result only in mishits and shots dragged suddenly to the floor. The louder the swish – the greater the power!

Thinking Point : Am I making full use of my wrist?

Eye

Here again there are three vital points to check:

1 Watch the shuttle every inch of the way from your opponent's racket to, onto, and just off your racket. 'Head down' is not just a golfing maxim! This gives clean hitting and few misses.

2 From the periphery of your eye learn to chart your opponents' court positions. This helps wise placement.

3 Watch too your opponent's hitting action and particularly the speed, angle and direction of the racket face in the crucial foot before impact. Observe its speed to tell you whether the shuttle will travel far and fast or short and slow; its angle to tell you whether the shuttle will go up or down; its direction to tell whether it is to forehand or backhand. Learn to 'read' your opponents' action (it is as slow and difficult a business – but just as rewarding – as reading was in your infancy). Then you will move to the

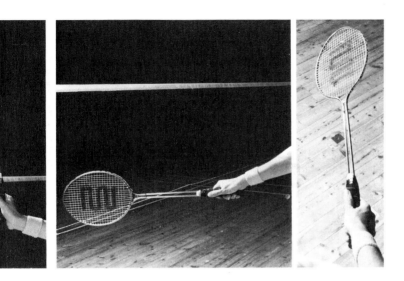

shuttle *as, or even before, the shuttle is hit.* There for the observing is the virtue of speed! *Practise this consciously every time you play.* Fail to concentrate, and no message is flashed by eyes to feet!
Thinking Point : Thoughtful use of the eye gives three virtues :
Consistency; Placement; Speed.

Body

In all strokes use that body to effect, Samantha! For power shots overhead, bend back and turn sideways to the net in the back-swing; spiral the body upright and square to the net for impact. Even in net-shots and low service sway the body gently into the shot. Keep on balance for a fast recovery.
Thinking Point : Correct body movement gives power, control and recovery.

Footwork

Feet come last but are very, very far from least. Indeed so impor-tant are they that they almost deserve the luxury of a short section all to themselves. Think of them at all times: as they wait for,

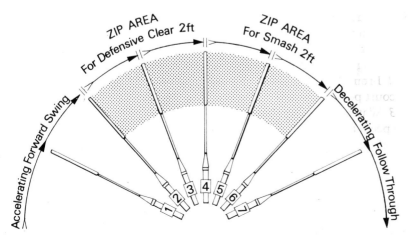

Diagram 2: Points of impact and zip areas for the clears and the smash: 1 & 2 the forward swing 3 impact for a defensive clear 4 impact for an attacking clear 5 impact for the smash 6 & 7 the follow-through.

Overleaf: **Diagram 3:** Footwork. 1 position of readiness 2 overhead smash, clear and drop 3 overhead backhand clear and drop 4 backhand drive, push and net shot 5 forehand drive, push and net shot 6 under-hand backhand lob and net shot 7 underhand forehand lob and net shot 8 dab and net shot. (Shuttles show points of impact.)

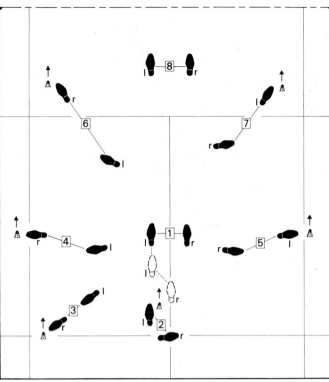

Ray Rofe (Kent) in full flight shows body suppleness and strength as he plays a round the-head stroke. Note his eyes fixed on the shuttle!

The position of readiness. The player is well-balanced, alert, and holds the racket-head to the right of the body and at shoulder height, ready to attack.

play and recover from a shot. They are the spring-board of all movement; the essential firm platform for accurate stroke production; the jet propulsion of attack and recovery.

Size 10½ or no, Sam, it is your feet that must get you *early* to the shuttle to attack it, to hit it down that *split second* before it finds comparative safety mere inches below the tape.

Between strokes stand square to the net in your position of readiness, knees bent, shoulder width apart, racket angled up across the stomach in defence, just in front of the right shoulder in attack, eyes observantly watching your opponents' positioning and stroking. Above all, be on the *balls* of your feet, constantly shifting, swaying, shuffling, dancing: a picture of restless mobility. Anything to overcome the drag of initial body inertia. For heaven's sake don't be shy about this, Samantha. Not after I've seen you living it up on the disco floor to 'The Hustle'! And when you start, Sam, do your best to give a very fair representation of a racing-car burning rubber. Move!

No, I'm not asking you to rival Sonia Lannaman. No 100 metre sprint for you – just a three metre dash! Stop – turn – dash – bend – stop – twist – dash – turn – stretch – dash – that's badminton movement. Drive off with short, low thrusting steps; pull up smartly on balance with a longer braking stride; and then, instant driving recovery. Never over-run the shuttle. *One* step too many backwards or forwards is really *two* steps lost, isn't it?

Running *backwards* can be woman's downfall on court, Samantha. *Run* backwards or chassé backwards (that is skip backwards bringing one foot up to the other). Sure, it's not a natural means of locomotion so *it must be practised at every opportunity*, off court and on. Never let the shuttle get behind you!

If you move neatly, lightly, Samantha, you should arrive at your rendezvous with the shuttle poised, on-balance and unruffled and totally in command of the situation. You cannot play either powerful or accurate shots if you are still running or off-balance or with feet wrongly positioned. Try to be stationary as you hit the shot. For overhead and underarm shots the stance is usually with the left foot forward pointing to the net, feet shoulder-width apart (except in the lob), knees slightly bent or straightening. For sidearm strokes adopt a longer stride with the feet parallel to the net (with the right foot leading for the backhand and the left for the forehand).

Two final points. Your eye is your accelerator; observe speed, direction and elevation of the shuttle *as it leaves your opponent's racket* – not as it crosses the net. Move then! Lust for the kill and hatred in the heart are the essential sparks to speed you off – whooooooosh!

Thinking Point : Split seconds count! Move early : Move fast.

Above: Speedy footwork is an essential ingredient of all stroke-play.

Below left: Steve Wassell (Hampshire) shows the need not only for power from the rear court but also for instant balanced recovery.

Below: Lynne Bladen epitomizes the lightness, ease and grace of badminton.

Chapter Six
Throw That Racket!

So much for the preliminaries. Now, at last, let's go on court.

Bring some shuttles on court – but not your racket. Patience, Samantha! First you are going to throw shuttles, then rackets – because to make life easy Providence ordained that the strokes you are going to learn are all a form of throwing. Simply remember an overarm throw is the *upward and forward snapping straight* of a bent arm and wrist (as in throwing a ball or a stone). *It is not a flat, bent-arm push or dab at head level.*

Right, have a go . . . Not too bad, but swing the arm more fully back and bend it more – that's better. And push the heel of the hand *upwards* at the ceiling not flat at the walls. Be rhythmic, relaxed. Throw! Throw! Throw!

Overarm Strokes

Fine, put the shuttle down and at long last take up that racket to 'shadow' the main strokes – play them without a shuttle to get the feel of them. Position of readiness! Check your grip. Left foot and shoulder forward so that you're sideways to the net. Sway your body-weight onto the back foot and at the same time bring the racket straight up and drop it down over your shoulder. Your arm is bent double; elbow up. And your wrist is fully cocked back. If it wasn't, you wouldn't be able to scratch the small of your back with the racket head. Inelegant perhaps – but effective, yes! Yes, actually tap your back – it's the only way you *know* the arm is fully bent. That's the *backswing.*

Above: Flemming Delfs just before impact. He is well-balanced with the wrist just about to uncock, the arm straightening from the 'back-scratch', eye on the shuttle and the left arm up as a sighter and counterbalance.

Below: Points of impact for: (left to right) the defensive (high) clear, the attacking (flat) clear, the drop shot, the smash.

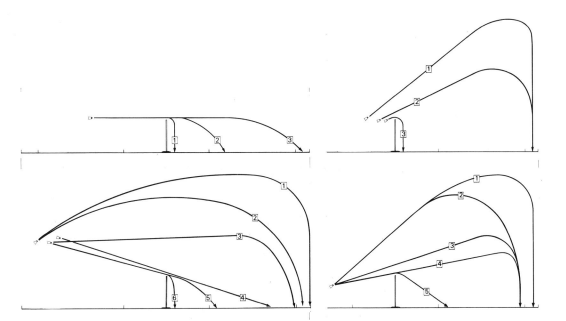

You can, if you prefer, sweep the racket-head firmly down past your legs and then, bending the arm outwards, bring the elbow up as in a tennis serve or a cricket throw. It takes a fraction longer – but do what comes naturally and effectively. Make sure your left arm comes up as a counter-balance.

Now, without pause, into the *forward swing*. Snap the arm (not the wrist yet) up straight – feel it – as your weight sways forward and your body turns at the hips square to the net. Uncock your wrist *only just before* the arm fully straightens.

For *impact*, hit into and through the shuttle, aiming the racket at your target and keeping it on line as long as you can before it sweeps down to the left of the body in the follow through and the right foot comes naturally forward. Badminton life is largely a matter of timing i.e. actually hitting the shuttle as the racket-head achieves maximum velocity.

No, don't just stand there – there's always another stroke to be played. So a quick *recovery* to your base and the 'ready position'.

Underarm Strokes

These are played with virtually the overhead action, but underarm. Try it. This time though sweep the racket *down* past your feet and up behind you so that, with bent arm, the racket head is just behind and to the right of your head. That's it! Now sweep down and forward – heel of hand leading, arm straightening, wrist un-cocking late, body weight swaying forward and square, racket on target all the time. Follow through up and across body, high in front of left shoulder.

Sidearm Strokes

Sidearm strokes are the same action in a different plane. No trouble! Like skimming a stone across water.

Diagram 4: Trajectories of strokes. *Top left*: Sidearm strokes. 1 net shot 2 half-court push 3 drive.
Top right: Underarm strokes. 1 high defensive lob 2 low attacking lob 3 net shot.
Bottom left: Overhead strokes. 1 very high clear 2 defensive high clear 3 attacking flat clear 4 smash 5 fast drop shot 6 slow (floating) drop shot.
Bottom right: Serves. 1 high singles serve 2 high doubles serve 3 flick serve 4 drive serve 5 low serve.

Chapter Seven
Basic Strokes

High Serve

Let's start with the high serve, Samantha. Why? Partly because it's easier than the low, but largely because it's a means of placing the shuttle in the air ('feeding') so that Sam can practise overhead shots. (Until you're fairly proficient you can 'hand feed', i.e. throw the shuttle. Even that is a way of practising a shot, isn't it?)

The high serve is a pleasant, flowing shot in which you crack the shuttle high and deep to the long service line. Hit it high to make timing difficult and deep to force your opponent as far back in court as you can and to blunt his smash as much as possible. But having said that it's still a defensive, upward stroke.

Thinking Point : Never hit up unless forced to as it gives your opponent the chance to hit down, to attack. Length, *then, is all!*

Right, you know what's wanted and why. You've shadowed the stroke. So now all you need think about is timing.

Hold the feathers between thumb and forefinger, vertical, at shoulder-height with your arm slightly bent, so that the shuttle is a foot forward of and to the right of your left foot. Relax, relax! Hold it – don't rush! Look at your target – the singles long service line. But pin-point it more: 18 inches from the centre line.

Ready again! Swing the racket back and at the start of the forward swing release the shuttle and simultaneously throw the racket head at it. Missed! Never mind, you'll miss plenty more. Everyone does. Remember the shuttle falls slowly like the feathers it is, so start your downward swing slowly, accelerating

The high serve (singles). Relaxed, unhurried and with the racket held high, Gillian selects her target; always watch that shuttle!; the wrist is just about to uncock and the body is turning; there is a very high follow-through to attain great height; finally, Gillian recovers to a position of readiness that is slightly towards the side to which the shuttle has been hit.

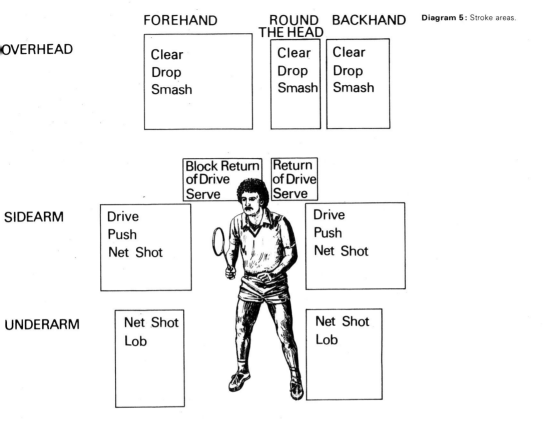

OVERHEAD

FOREHAND

| Clear |
| Drop |
| Smash |

ROUND THE HEAD

| Clear |
| Drop |
| Smash |

BACKHAND

| Clear |
| Drop |
| Smash |

| Block Return of Drive Serve | Return of Drive Serve |

SIDEARM

| Drive |
| Push |
| Net Shot |

| Drive |
| Push |
| Net Shot |

UNDERARM

| Net Shot |
| Lob |

| Net Shot |
| Lob |

gradually to maximum speed at impact.

Thinking Point : Maximum racket head speed at impact *(not before or after) gives maximum shuttle velocity*

Missed again. Never worry. Imprint the target area in your mind's eye, then watch the shuttle only and see it hit the strings. Keep your head down. If you look up to see where it's gone before you hit it – there won't be anything to see. Now, slowly!

Well done! More length needed though. So hit a little harder and push the racket head farther through. Better! A little more height now so uncock the wrist a shade more, and crisply. Good but off-target. Aim the racket head at the target throughout.

Finally, the last point to remember is to make the follow-through more pronounced so that shuttle and strings are in contact as long as possible.

So practise – but concentrate on one point at a time.

Defensive Clear

Half an hour's worked wonders. Now for a complementary stroke – the clear. This is another defensive stroke because it hits the shuttle high and deep from one baseline to the other. Like the high serve, it is used a lot in singles, sparingly in men's or ladies' doubles, rarely in mixed. The height gives you time to recover back to base. It's a full-blooded, pleasing overhead stroke – a useful insurance policy. More, it's the basis of the two overhead

The defensive clear. Gillian Gilks swings from a full backswing to make contact with her arm straight and her body slightly turned and at full stretch. After impact there is an instant recovery back to centre base.

attacking strokes, the smash and the drop-shot, that we are going to practise later.

Samantha, take up your position between the two back-lines because that's where it's generally played from. Hi! Don't just stand like a traffic warden on point duty – bounce!

Thinking Point : Except for service and return, feet should never be still.

Sam, come up to the front service line and serve high to the base-line, a singles service. Aim for the right shoulder. Good feeding from you makes Samantha's task easier – gives her time and makes running unnecessary. Samantha, just a few practice shadow shots. Relax! Full swing! Throw! Fine!

Missed! All right, it's not a crime. Simply, you were half an hour too late, because of rusty reflexes. Swing back *early*. As a beginner, you'll find you need to swing back slowly as Sam starts his forward swing. As your sense of timing develops, you'll be able to swing back later – but never swing hurriedly.

Contact! Well done! But contact at head height with bent arm like one of the Seven Dwarfs! Don't let the shuttle *drop*, Samantha. Reach *up*! Contact! But the result is all height and no length, way short of the base-line and wide open to instant slaughter. Make impact a little further forward, just over your head (not behind it), so with racket-head at 45° you get maximum length with height. Push the heel of the hand up. Try again. Two feet gained! Drop the racket right down your back. Scratch – and up! Better again. This time forget you're a lady – thump it. Improving! Now use a crisper, last-second wrist action. Above all, swing back early!

Thinking point : Power is an amalgam of good balance, full arm snap, strong wrist uncocking and body sway which together give maximum acceleration at impact.

Attacking Overheads

Two weeks later, after much toil, sweat, tears and thought have given you the basics of playing the clear, let's introduce you to its big brothers: the drop shot (and the reply to it – the lob or under-arm clear) and the smash (and the reply to it – the return of smash). You must play the clear, drop shot and smash with just the same action for deception. Make them identical so that your opponent doesn't know until the last second what's going to hit him – or where.

Thinking Point : Brain must direct brawn.

Drop Shot (Slow or Floating)

We'll take the drop shot first because it's a simpler lead-in to the hitting-*down* action in the smash that often causes some difficulty. The clear drove your opponent back so now we want a stroke that draws him in. So it's a gentle, deceptive, overhead attacking shot that drops the shuttle downward as close to the net as possible. Certainly no further back than the front service line. Don't use it in mixed doubles.

Thinking Point : An attacking shot is any shot, no matter how gently played, that forces opponents to lift.

Practise a few clears first. Fine! Now use just the same action, but this time slow down wrist and arm action in the last two feet before impact which is now just in front of the head with the wrist coming gently through and over. Got the hang of it? Then let's go! Is that a half-hearted clear or a strong drop, Sam? Cut down the village blacksmith touch and take it high too, rather than letting it drop. No, Sam! You've gone to the other extreme of delicacy. A dab with no backswing is as good as a telegram saying 'Here she comes, boys! Please meet.' And they will! Full swing,

The lob. Gillian Gilks swings the racket back early and takes a long lunge to make contact with the shuttle. After the follow-through there is the vital instant drive back to base.

27

please, Sam. Good, that's more deceptive! But, now you're hitting it up – not down. Yes, I'm fully aware it fell two feet closer to the net. The snag is that Samantha could have gone home for tea and biscuits and still been in time to crack it down! Hit down, Sam, and hurry her. Push through; keep it on the strings for control. Gently! Better – better – better . . . shorter . . . shorter.

Lob

You're getting tired of picking up shuttles you say, Samantha? All right then, have a go at playing the reply to a drop-shot; the lob or under-arm clear. Watch while Gillian demonstrates . . . What did you notice? Hole in one! It's simply the high serve played at full stretch with a lunge. Have a go! Remember length and height are of more value than pearls . . . well, if you say so, Samantha. It's a woman's world! To get good length bring the racket back as you run in and don't just hopefully jab it forward from the front foot. If you rush in too close to the shuttle you'll tie yourself in knots so lunge to the shuttle and take it alongside the leading foot. And once you've played the shot don't stop to admire it. Push back to recover fast.

Smash

This is the big day! Last and by far the best of the overheads – the smash. This power-stroke is the major point-winner and so your staunchest ally. And for good measure let's throw in the defensive push return, the smash's complementary stroke.

Sam, action stations on the back doubles service line. Always smash lobs and clears short of that line; little from behind it because a shuttle decelerates very quickly. No, Samantha, this is not just a stroke for the men. Petite ladies (Fiona Smith or Gill Gowers) as well as long-legged ones (Gillian Gilks) can, with timing, training and wrist, play a very mean smash. Besides shuttle *speed* is not all.

Steepness runs it a close second. A flat smash can be returned downwards with interest; a steep one, even if not a winner, forces a lift so you're still in with a big chance. Aim for the knees!

Placement, too, doubles the smash's effectiveness: be able to put it into a gap for a winner or into the body for a cramped return that in doubles your partner at the net can destroy. No brainless bashing onto the racket. Marry pace to precision! *Consistency* too! One scorcher doesn't make up for one into and another under the net. Never let your game be splintered with error.

So if you're in difficulty, off-balance or out of breath play it cool!

Thinking Point : Always play the percentages.

Sam, there's latent power there, but your smashes are flatter than yesterday's beer. You're a coach's nightmare. All three cardinal sins together! Impact above the head; bent arm; no wrist action. Let's cure impact first: dance, don't saunter, to that shuttle and get *behind* it. Correct impact is vital: it should be 18 inches *in front of you*. That's more like it! Now the bent arm. Swing back

earlier to give yourself time both to swing back fully and to throw
your racket up to hit the shuttle, straight-armed, at the highest
possible point to give your smash steepness. Have a go! Up . . .
up . . . up! That's more like it. Now add a slightly stronger uncocking of the wrist. The greater the swish; the greater the power.
Remember? Holy smoke! I swear those three all hit your own feet.
You'll be joining the walking wounded, Sam, if you snatch *too*
wristily at it. Moderation . . ! Fine! Placement, alas, noticeable
only by its absence. You're spraying shuttles round like machine-
gun bullets. Just *aim* the racket at that tempting target. Curl the
racket-head over the shuttle to bring it *down*. Don't cut it! That
reduces speed. Hit it squarely with the full face of the racket. Hit
into it and through it!

Return of Smash

You bruise easily, Samantha? No need to. Just wear our smash-
proof defensive push. As soon as you've served, be on your toes,
mid-court. You can't trust him – that smash may be a drop or a
clear (unintentionally at this stage; intentionally later). Right?
So . . . get into the position of readiness; eyes analytically watching

The return of smash. From an alert defensive position of readiness Pedro Blach plays a limited backswing to take the shuttle high and early with bent arm and a firm wrist. Finally there is a short follow-through.

The drive. This sequence shows the player: moving across; swinging the racket back with his eyes still on the shuttle; bringing the right foot across to lean into the shuttle while simultaneously straightening his arm; returning to base after the stroke has been played.

the racket-head direction. You have only a split second to see the shuttle so pick up the line of flight as it's hit! No time for flowing backswings or follow-through. Nine inches is about the maximum for each. Then, leaning into it (with unblinking serenity) play a bent-arm push with a firm wrist and the racket-face slightly open. Make it skim the net: fast enough to beat the net-player yet slow enough to draw in the smasher. That way he doesn't get a second bite at the cherry!

Sheer self-defence, Samantha, but quite good. Keep those feet moving or you'll send down roots. Remember, move in a foot or so to take the smash a little earlier if you can. Better, but now you're stabbing at it like a drunken fencer. *See* it early. Slow it down. Push, don't jab. Keep the racket face open. Satisfying, isn't it to throw everything back at him?

Other Strokes

Now let's have a crack at a side-arm stroke, the *drive*. A power shot, cousin, three times removed, of the push. Use it when the shuttle is just above net-height, too low for a smash but still begging to be hit hard. It's played mainly by the man in mixed doubles from near the side lines and some 7 feet to 11 feet behind the front service line. A cracker of a shot! To feed, hit the shuttle to that area some two to three feet above the net as it crosses it. Remember, Sam this is a long curved flinging action. As a beginner, it's easier with the left foot across; later you'll probably put the right foot across to save time. Have a go. To hit it straight down the side-line make impact just in front of the body and only half uncock the wrist . . . Not bad at all but you're lifting. Oh yes, I know it's only a foot or so but that's enough for it to be counter-attacked: remember that a good drive travels fast and flat or even a little down. It's the old, old, cry: 'Swing back earlier to take it tape high'. Also close the racket-face, i.e. lessen the angle of the

The backhand net 'kill'. Gillian Gilks uses her reach to begin a restricted back-swing early and dab down wristily for a winner without hitting the net.

racket-head to the shuttle. Again, don't cut! That's better but lean into it more!

How can you hit it cross-court for variety? Easy enough! Simply play it some two feet earlier.

Now, your turn, Samantha. Yes, although most commonly played by the man in mixed doubles, the drive can be used in ladies' doubles too. As with the smash, hit into the body or a gap, but remember a drive can boomerang – coming back at you nearly as fast as it left. And you'll find, all in good time, that the back-hand drive can easily be adapted into a lady's speciality shot: the 'Danish Wipe' or 'Swedish Swish'! Intriguing? More later.

Net Shots

Now you know a bit about the drive your mixed partner will play frequently, let's have a look at *net shots*, which are the woman's forte in mixed, Samantha. I hesitate to state the obvious – they're played from near the net, up or down. Take both as high and as early as you can.

Let's take *hitting down* first. Stand midway between net and front service line, square to the net, knees slightly bent, racket vertical in either basic or frying-pan grip just in front of you at tape-height, elbow bent. Sam will hit shuttles gently up to you a foot or so above tape height from mid-court. All you need do is dab them down – extend the forearm and slightly uncock the wrist. Remember: it's against the laws to play the shuttle before it crosses the net, or for you even to touch the net . . . My God, let alone dismantle it like that! No follow-through here; stop your racket dead, then bring it instantly up to the ready position again. No time for any back-swing.

Better – but don't stretch for it. Move – get behind it! That one took you in the throat, did it? Then bend your knees and sink down a little. Keep the racket *at* tape-height. Uncock the wrist

Service faults. The Author, suitably fortified, had to force himself into these unwonted excesses! The illustrations show (left to right): a foot on the line; the back foot off the floor; the shuttle above the waist; the racket-head clearly above the racket-hand.

more to bring the shuttle down steep and short; if you don't, it's all too easy to crack the plaster on the back wall. That's it, Sam; keep them coming back with a wristless, pendulum push.

Now, for a change, to second-best *upward net shots*. For self-preservation they must almost literally crawl over the net to drop straight down on the other side. Hit them too high and it will be your opponent's turn to dab down to good effect.

So, same position as before, Samantha, but if you're using the frying-pan grip you'll have to practise a quick change to basic grip. Make it a perfect shot in miniature. No, no! You're just letting it bounce off the racket. You must *play* a complete stroke. Nine inches looped back and forward swing, impact and a three-inch follow-through. Take it tape high. Racket up, up . . . Whoa! Now you've gone mad: don't stab and jab. Watch it; slow it down, play a stroke; ease it over, don't thump it; sway into it; concentrate; take care! Much better. Now you're really using your woman's silken touch!

Net shots are used by both men and women in all three branches of the game. And as a bonus they're the basis of vital service returns.

Low Service

Neither the low service nor its return is a power stroke – and yet they are 50% of the game. Serve well: points flow. Receive well: your opponents can't score.

Here's another glorious opportunity for that woman's touch of yours, Samantha. But first the server's Six Commandments:

Thou shalt not:

1 Have a foot on the line;

2 Lift either foot clear of the floor;

3 Delay unduly; or hit the feathers before the base;

4 Feint: i.e. stop then start the stroke again;

5 Have any part of the shuttle above waist-height;

6 Have any part of the racket-head above any part of the racket-hand at impact.

Learn them! All are important but breach of 5 or 6 in particular will render even you, Samantha, as unpopular as a taxman. It is all too easy to break those laws quite unwittingly so ask your best friend – better still, your worst! – to vet you occasionally.

Stand as you did for the high serve. The purpose of the low serve is to make the shuttle drop just before it crosses the net, to skim it and to land a foot beyond the front service line near the junction with the centre line. So think for a moment. What have we got to alter?

'Less power? So racket and shuttle are closer together initially?' Dead right, Samantha. Lower the left arm slightly and bend it more; now the shuttle is chest high and will drop alongside the forward left foot. And the racket head is down just behind and to the right of the right thigh.

'Elevation is virtually nil . . . so there should be less use of the wrist?' Smack on the nose, Sam. So what you need now, Saman-tha, is a simple, gentle, pendulum push action with the heel of the hand leading and the *wrist cocked back* throughout. Watch Gillian first then it's all yours . . .

Hold it! You're all of a twitch! Relax – shake the arm and fingers supple. Grip with a gentle firmness and check your arm is well bent. Slow it down! The shuttle drifts down like a feather; hit too fast and you're there before it is! Look at your two targets first: net-tape and floor. Keep your opponent waiting. Now con-centrate on the shuttle. Ease it, coax it, caress it, push it over the net. Be confident. Sway into it! Fine – that's slower, lower, smoother.

One or two have steepled up, haven't they? That means you're either holding the shuttle too far forward or you've got a touch of beginner's wrist twitch. Nasty complaint! Alter the racket head's angle of elevation but a fraction and the result is a terrifyingly disproportionate amount of shuttle-rise above the tape. Have another go . . . Better, much better, but you're dropping too many into the wrong court. One fault – perhaps three or four points

The low serve (doubles). Standing near the T-junction Gillian Gilks, wrist cocked back, swaying forward and with limited backswing, carefully strokes the shuttle just above the tape. She then instantly advances, racket up, to cut off any net return.

Above: Front and side-view of the stance for receiving serve. This is an aggressive dominating stance right up to the line! The player is balanced on the balls of his feet with his weight thrown slightly forward and his racket kept well up as he observantly watches the server's action.

Right: The backhand smash. This is never as fast as the forehand smash and so must be played nearer to the net.

wasted with one careless stroke. Take *care* as well as *time*. Aim the racket at the target, but leave a margin for error. (You're not Nora Perry yet!) Keep shuttle-strings in contact for as long as possible. Follow through to waist height.

Return of Service

Your main aim, Sam, is to meet the shuttle early – with murderous intent – in order to hit down. It's yours too, Samantha – more so, for lifting service is too often a woman's weakness.

Position yourself about five feet from the front service line and eight feet from the back doubles service line; in the right court 18 inches from the centre-line; in the left about three feet. From there you are about equidistant from impact with low and high serves. Every week, try to move in a couple of inches until eventually you are toeing the line – yet still able to get back to attack the high serve.

Now for *Poise* or stance. Stand a little less like the Statue of Liberty, Sam; that's better. Get your opponent in your sights and crouch. Left knee well bent, right leg at stretch behind. On the balls of your feet. Weight slightly forward. Racket at head height. Look menacing! And above all watch the server's racket. There lie the clues to where and how you will have to run.

So to *power*, for the *push-off*. You won't have to run more than three yards so it's not so much a matter of 'run like hell' as of 'push-off early like lightning'. Try to meet every low serve chest-high in front of the front service line. Never, never wait for the shuttle to come to you and so be forced to lift. Similarly, be able to rocket back in time to hit down. Read the serve; be jet-propelled! But remember: no profligate waste of careless shots into the net or out of court. Just a reminder though, Sam, before you turn into a kind of human Catherine Wheel, a second Kevin Jolly.

The backhand lob. When playing this stroke begin your backswing early and make sure that your right foot, shoulder and elbow are pointing to the shuttle as here. Compare this stroke with the forehand lob on page 27.

The backhand drive. Compare this with the forehand drive on page 29. Note full swing, straight arm and point of impact.

Know the laws applying to the return of service. Only four. (Answers on p. 36).

The actual returns? In order of preference, low serve returns are: a crisp dab down; a deceptive half-court push that lands near the sideline between server and partner; a tight upward net shot; a deceptive lob to the backhand. High serves: a smash; a drop.

Backhands

  1 Use the backhand grip.
  2 Point the right foot and elbow into the shuttle:
    For the backhand lob: right foot forward, elbow down.
    For the backhand drive: right foot across, elbow tape high.
    For the backhand overheads: right foot to back corner, elbow up.
  3 For each stroke at the end of the backswing the right hand is near the left shoulder.
  4 Power again comes from snapping straight a bent arm and cocked wrist in a *wide*, flinging arc.

A weak backhand will cost you dear! Your opponent will attack yours as relentlessly as you should hammer his!

Thinking Point: Practise all backhands at least as much as forehands.

35

Chapter Eight
More Advanced Strokes

Never try to run before you can walk. Use, practise and perfect the strokes described in the last chapter; they will give you a firm foundation. Then, gradually, introduce these more advanced strokes one by one. They'll bring interest and sting to your game. Add them to your repertoire in roughly this order then gradually you'll have an answer to every problem.

Flick Serve

An essential complement to the low serve rather than a luxury. A joyous means of taming the fierce rusher of serves. Like the high serve, it forces the receiver back but unlike the high serve it hides its intent and so hurries – and worries – the receiver.

The stroke is no great problem to learn. Do two or three low serves exactly as before. Right, in comes bully-boy receiver getting rather too big for his Dunlop 'Green Flash'. All that's needed to tame the brute, Samantha, is a touch of the usually forbidden fruit – the strong uncocking of the wrist in the last fraction of a second to zip the shuttle to the back of the court *just* over his agonisedly upstretched racket.

Try it out, Samantha . . . Fine, except your publicity department is working overtime; you're using a noticeably longer and faster swing. Not only is it unnecessary (the wrist alone can do the trick) but it warns the observant receiver of your evil intentions. Essential surprise is lost. Don't look covertly at the back-line and don't lengthen or shorten your preparation time; indeed, there should seem to be no difference at all from the low serve. Do two low serves then start a third with the same intent but *just before impact* crisply uncock the wrist. And think for yourself where best to place it. (Answers on p. 39).

Drive Serve

And now the drive. Another service variation; another wolf in sheep's clothing! It's frequently played by the man in mixed doubles. Again do two or three low serves, however this time, just before impact, keep the wrist cocked back but jab fast forward with the forearm for extra zip. Result? A *flat*, fast serve that was through your opponent's defences before she could blink. Take more care; pin-point your target. Then we shan't have two out at the back with one in the wrong court.

Knowing you're a bit of a gambler, Sam, how can you make the drive a still more barbed weapon – even at some risk? Yes, in the right hand court you can widen the angle by serving wide from the sideline, but you are sadly out of position and so must have good mutual understanding as to who takes which return.

Thinking Point : The later the change : The greater the deception.

Answers to question on page 35: Keep both feet on the ground; don't move before the shuttle is struck; no feints or distracting movements; no undue delay.

Round-the-Head Strokes

Like all great generals you must invent new weapons to counter new attacks. In this respect the flick doesn't present any new problems because if you are quick enough then it's easy to apply pressure with smash or drop shot. The drive is altogether another matter to defend against. The dab block-shot, taken just in front of the head and hit down to the corner of the net is useful but not aggressive enough. That's where round-the-head shots come in.

Let's deal with high shuttles. Some towering serves to the backhand corner, please, Sam. Now, instead of turning lazily to play a backhand clear, Samantha, move quickly so that the shuttle is only a foot or so to your left. Lean over to that side and clear with the

Far left: The block-shot. The shuttle is taken just in front of the head and dabbed down to a corner of the net.

Left: Kevin Jolly (Essex and England) seizes a fleeting chance by smashing powerfully round-the-head rather than by using a weaker backhand.

37

Above: The round-the-head smash off a drive serve. Note the left foot splayed out for balance and the crisp backswing. Impact takes place to the left and just in front of the head.

Above right: Steen Skovgaard (Denmark), quizzically watched by Delfs, displays a round-the-head shot played at an unusually low level to maintain the attack. Again the left foot is out for balance, the forearm is brushing the head and contact is well to the left of the head.

usual forehand action. But your forearm, instead of being directly over your right shoulder, will be above or even to the left of your head. Lean well over. Put your left foot out still more to the left to help you maintain balance. Then, after playing the stroke, push-off strongly for quick recovery. Round-the-head strokes take the pressure off a not very robust backhand, give greater power and put you back into circulation faster.

All right, Samantha, I know I said the drive must be *flat* so let's adapt. Drive serves this time, please, Sam. So quickly out again with that left foot, Samantha. (Yes, you may step into your partner's court) whip the racket back, bend the arm and bring the forearm flat across, just grazing the head. Impact (with the racket face slightly closed) is well to the left of and just in line with your head. That's right! Hammer it into the server's body but look out for an equally quick return which can be lethal if you haven't recovered balance. To hit cross-court, you'll have to make impact a fraction earlier. Hit it late and side-line spectators have to duck!

Danish Wipe or Swedish Swish

Delightfully expressive names, aren't they? Indicative of the fact that this stroke was pioneered largely by beautiful Nordic girls who like Samantha (don't preen yourself yet) weren't exactly at their best with the overhead backhand clear, and who really hit it!

High lobs to the backhand corner, please, Sam. Move smartly across to it, Samantha, as though for a backhand drive. Remember, right foot across and racket well back behind the left shoulder. Let the shuttle *drop*! A sign of good coaching, I suppose, that you tried to take it early but just for once ignore your finer feelings – *and let it drop*. Now try again! Instead of hitting flat at tape height bend the knees a little, sweep the racket-head down and then up and under to lift the shuttle fast to the base-line. Height? Depends on circumstances.

Thinking Point: Hit high only when you need time to regain base.

Backhand Serve

While we're backhand conscious let's take a quick look at the backhand serve. A useful variant, it comes in three guises: low, flick and drive.

Bring your right foot up to the service line and your left hand down and outstretched holding the shuttle just below waist height. Right elbow up at shoulder height so that the arm is bent. Bring your right hand down (no, I'm not a driving instructor, Sam) so that the racket is vertical some 18 inches in front of the stomach, but just behind the shuttle. Draw the racket back to the stomach, then, in the same motion simply extend the forearm (wrist cocked back, of course) and hitting it almost out of the hand, push the shuttle over. Follow through on line and quickly raise the racket into attack position. Couldn't be simpler! The backswing can vary: Indonesians restrict it to a mere six inches; other players sweep the racket well back under the left arm. Try all three types.

Defence

If you always play a push return even the dullest opponent will soon prepare for it. So, like aces up the sleeve, use these four variants from well-chosen time to time. They're all based on strokes already practised so now it's action rather than words.

Net Return: For use in singles, play just like the push but take the speed off by relaxing your grip and with minimal swing play a dead-racket shot.

Drive Return; Quick eye and reflexes are needed here. Don't just push; drive flat and fast cross-court or into the smasher's body.

Lob Return: Simply lift deep to the back of the court in a war of attrition. Up . . . up . . . up! Had the crowd cheering on their feet, didn't you? But you're still defending . . . so use it mainly to sap energy or, by hitting fairly low to the corners, to hurry opponents into error.

Wrist Flick: Played so well by the Indonesians. No backswing, but a strong wrist action only, fast and low to the corners.

Answer to question on page 36: Aim for the outside corners, which gives these advantages: the greater diagonal distance means the initial speed can be greater without flying out of court; the receiver is driven farther from his base; the receiver may be badly positioned or off-balance as he hits his return.

Ray Sharp (Kent and England) at the end of a long backswing. The shuttle is below waist level and the right foot is near to but not touching the line. Alan Connor, his partner, is in an alert defensive position.

The jump smash is used to gain extra height for a steep return. It needs fitness though!

Dab

Note this one well, Samantha. It's the risk *you* have to take if either of you lift in mixed. Crouch on the front service line, cross-court to the smasher, racket in front of, or just to the right of your face. Dab (down, if you can). Highly rewarding against the flat smasher, but sheer hell against the steep one, isn't it? Lynx-eye instant reflexes and steel nerves are needed here. It's the nearest thing known to hari-kari – and you'll have the scars to prove it!

Net Returns

Cool it! Slow down the tempo and live longer. Let's add a few intriguing net-shot variations to your repertoire.

Brush: Players, lemming-like, often rush serve after serve into the net at very considerable point expenditure. Either they just don't realize that en route the shuttle has dropped fractionally below tape-height or else an upward net shot to them is like showing the white feather.

A perceptive alternative is to crouch a little to get under the shuttle. Then brush the racket face forwards and up and across the shuttle base. Admittedly the shuttle still rises, but it drops quickly and the rotary motion of the racket adds a deceptive touch.

Stab: If you cut straight under the shuttle with the side of the frame leading, or stab under it with the top leading, the shuttle will somersault 'base over feathers'.

Cut: If you cut down the side of the base and around under it, the shuttle will both spin around on its vertical axis and also somersault. Hit correctly, the shuttle will brush the tape and topple over and straight down the net. Even if it doesn't, your opponent

40

must let the shuttle drop before attempting to hit it.

And finally (to end on a note of real hostility) back to the all-important attacking shots.

Above left: The forehand stab.

Above: The backhand stab.

Cut Smash

The cut smash is a valuable reply to a high serve and is played, as in tennis, by being hit down the side of the shuttle. Its good points are that the fast arm action yet slowed-down shuttle speed is highly deceptive, it makes the shuttle veer a little to the side-line and it drops much shorter than usual. Thus, it is useful in singles.

Jump Smash

As a grand finale – the jump smash, which is fascinating to watch, but is simply a straightforward smash played some 18 inches clear of the floor. The jump must be timed so that impact is at the top of it. Good balance on landing is essential for quick recovery.

Attacking Clear

The high clear already described is a defensive shot. It can easily be changed into an attacking one. Simply hit the shuttle with the racket tilted only very slightly upwards, just in front of the head. Thus the shuttle is hit, fast and flat but just high enough to avoid interception. Use it when your opponent is too far up court and you are both well-balanced and well-positioned.

Drop Shot (Fast or Attacking)

Simply take the shuttle 9–12 inches further forward, uncock the wrist a little more and hit, say, 50% harder. Hard enough to pass the lady in mixed (its chief use) but not hard enough to reach the man. Aim for those side-line gaps between your opponents to maintain the attack from the base-line.

Chapter Nine
Singles

Basic Tactics

Singles is a game for the fit (Hi! where are you off to, Sam?) . . . and for the patient. (And you, Samantha?) Reread 'fitness' in chapter three before proceeding further; a well-tuned body is essential for the singles game.

Always remember the three fundamentals:

1 As the court is longer (22 feet) than it is wide (17 feet) it is commonsense to run your opponent *up and down* into exhaustion or error or to create an opening.

2 For this purpose *length* is all-important; your clears and drops must be fully deep and short respectively.

3 Try to find your opponent's weaknesses and play on them relentlessly; try to prevent him attacking yours.

In the following tactical discussion do what I suggest often but not always, otherwise your opponent will be able to anticipate your painfully obvious pattern of play.

Thinking Point : Few rules are ever invariable.

Serving So, Sam, take up your position for serving near the centre-line and about four feet behind the front service line. Nearer still if necessary to make sure you get the vital length – within six inches of the base line. That, though, will mean you've immediately got to dance (I use the word advisedly) back to your general base which is astride the centre line some 12 feet from the net. Serve to the centre line (allow 18 inches margin for error) from the right court; to the backhand corner from the left. The latter not only attacks your opponent's backhand but also safeguards yours.

Diagram 6: Basic singles positions. B: General base S: Server R: Receiver. 1 and 2: base moved 18 inches towards the side to which the shuttle has been hit. 3: base is moved forward if a close net or drop-shot is played.

Service court area.

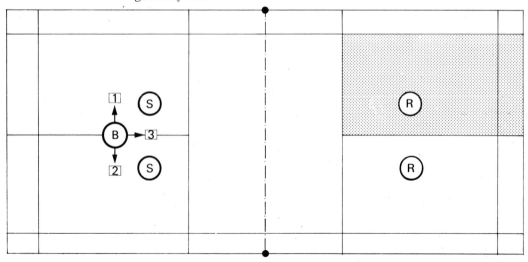

Receiving Now let's reverse positions. When you're receiving, Sam, stand about six feet from the service line and near the centre line in the right court but roughly in the centre of the left court. A rather more upright stance than the doubles 'tiger crouch' because you're going to be moving backwards more often than forwards.

General Pattern of Play Now, what kind of return shot will you play? Drops and clears? Quite right. Sometimes one; sometimes the other. If your clear is still weak and will only reach mid-court, it's best to play two or three drops first. Then with your opponent over-anticipating or well up court, even a weak clear may put him in trouble with the shuttle behind him. To the middle or to the corners? Of course to the corners. That makes your opponent run both further and more awkwardly. And especially to his Achilles heel – the deep backhand corner.

So there's the pattern – or rather, un-pattern; good length drops and clears to make openings and to force weak returns. Give these weak returns the full treatment – the smash, right into the body or into a gap. Never smash from deeper than the back service line because if you're off-balance a quick return will play havoc with your well-laid plans.

This is a war of attrition, play two or three clears – a drop – a clear – two or three drops – two or three clears, probably to the backhand. Each return (let's hope!) becomes weaker than the last. Never be in a hurry. Keep your opponent wriggling on the hook

Typical singles situations.
Above left: Rudi Hartono, many times All-England Singles Champion, un-hurriedly plays a backhand net-shot.
Above: Hartono takes early a tape-toppling net-shot while Delfs stays in expect-antly to kill a loose return.

until you're in a position to play a winning smash. Even that pattern will avail you little if your clears and drops are not deceptively alike.

Reverse positions again. Imagine you are now on the receiving end. How are you going to defend here, Samantha? Pin back her ears on the base-line with counter clears of still better length or play still tighter drop-shots? Drops returned deep with lobs? Smashes pushed back low? That's the idea, Samantha! And between shots? 'You know me, Coach – back to base like a flash. No hanging about admiring my own shots. Instant action: that's my maxim!

Right, then, on court. See if you can put the theory into practice.

More Advanced Tactics

Three months' training and practice have worked wonders for you both. So, to more advanced tactics. We'll take it stroke by stroke with the serve first.

Serving Using only the high serve sure does get mighty wearisome, Samantha! The remedy is simple: vary the height and the placement. Some real 'steeplers' (roof permitting); others hit just high enough to avoid interception. For placement variation, hit some to the centre line in the left hand court to narrow the angle of return.

If your opponent stands well back to receive or is strong overhead, slip in the occasional low serve – but only if your backhand is fireproof and can cope effectively with the ensuing blitz. And, if in anticipation she then moves in a couple of feet, drive her back with a strong flick or two. (You then have an extra $2\frac{1}{2}$ feet to play with.) Or what about a contra-flick? This is a high serve action, deceptively slowed into a low serve. Or, if her reflexes are rusty, or she leaves an obvious gap, try the occasional drive.

Below: Gillian Gilks, driven completely to the back of the court, plays a deceptive round-the-head drop shot to Margaret Beck who is intelligently positioned to attack any drop or clear.

Below right: Pedro Blach plays a push shot in response to a smash. Note that the racket-face is slightly open and that the player is leaning into the shot.

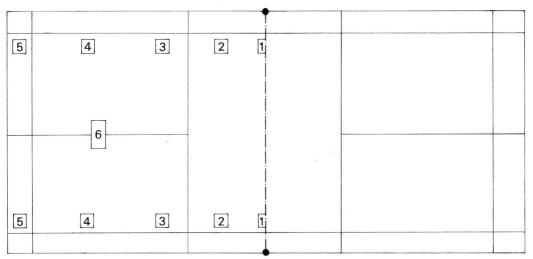

Putting on the Pressure Circuit training has done wonders for your speed and stamina, Sam, so let's hot up the tempo and be a bit more adventurous. Let's really push your opponent, giving him no respite to recharge his batteries. Let's put in the knife!

If, worried by your deceptive drops, your opponent lies a little too far up court, then play your clears and lobs faster and flatter. Drive yourself to take every shot earlier. If you can read his drops and so take them near tape-height rather than desperately digging them out of the floorboard grooves, then you can play net-shots, preferably stab ones because they tend to hug the net. This precludes a return, fast lob so you can afford to stay fairly close in to play another tight net shot or to knock off your opponent's not quite accurate return with a downward dab. And if you want to really push it – and your luck – take a leaf out of the Chinese book;

Diagram 7: Singles attack points. 1 net shots 2 drop shots 3 cut smashes 4 smashes 5 lobs and clears 6 a smash into the body.

Two views of Mike Tredgett (Gloucestershire and England). In both he is using his speed to take the shuttle early to hit down and hurry (and worry) his opponent into error.

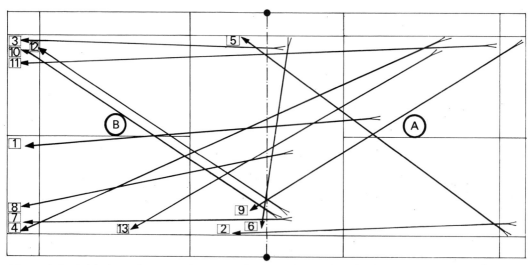

Diagram 8: A typical singles rally. The numbers show the sequence in which A played his strokes (B's returns are not shown). Can you read A's thoughts as he played each shot?

jump to play your drops and smashes. Drive your opponent into the ground! But only if you're really fit.

Smashing And talking of the smash – yes I know I'm doing most of it, Sam – why not unleash the big one more often now that it's got more than a hint of sonic boom? But it must be *steep* and hit the lines. And as a spin-off, the cut smash dropping short would be doubly effective, wouldn't it? Food for thought there!

Return of Smash For the sake of variety, to the half-court push return add the net return (almost dead racket) and for contrast, wrist-flick lob-drives.

Backhand Varied serves worrying your opponent now, Samantha? Yes? Why the worried look then? Oh, backhand trouble! Never worry, you're not the first. But if you don't do your wrist exercises and practise, your backhand is always going to be a sickly thing. Until then you'll have to settle for the Danish Wipe. Or better still, move, move, move! . . . and take more shots round-the-head but stay well-balanced, please.

Deception Anything else while you're here, Samantha? Good grief! *You* don't need *me* to tell you about that, do you? All right then, deception. Yes, you must use more and better deception if you're going to hobble a quick-footed opponent. You've got to be positively Machiavellian. Use your head – and wrist. I've already given you a lead – occasional flick and drive serves and cut smashes. Never overdo deception or it can lose its magic.

But you can still add 'held' shots to those I've mentioned. That means you keep your wrist cocked back in lobs and fast clears until the last foot before impact so that your opponent doesn't know whether your return will be to the net or to the rear court. Don't forget, too, to use last-second turns of the wrist to give wrong-footing change of direction. Beware though lest you are tempted to gild the lily with too much trickery. And lastly a very thorough check-up of your basic actions for all overhead shots. They must be identical.

Chapter Ten
Men's And Ladies' Doubles

Basic Tactics

Well, you two must part company temporarily on court for now we're going to play men's and ladies' doubles. But the tactics I'm going to explain apply equally to both branches of the game . . . except for a few variations in ladies' doubles that I'll whisper in your ear at the end, Samantha.

Positions In your tactical infancy be content to play strict sides; in other words, you and your partner are each responsible for covering all of one lengthways half of the court. Who takes the stroke down the middle? The player who can take it forehanded.

Then progress to a slightly wiser method of court-division. If your partner is a stranded whale at the net, obviously help him out by taking the deep lob or the clear over his head. Even as you go to the rescue with a ringing shout of 'Mine', he nips across to cover the half you have vacated. He'll return the compliment when you're stranded at the back.

These systems have the virtue of simplicity when (in the early days) your mind is too fully occupied merely with hitting the shuttle to be able to spare even a cell or two of it for tactics. Admittedly, they give you a sound grounding in movement and defensive tactics but are weak in attack. So, as soon as you can, graduate to the system outlined in 'More Advanced Tactics'. Then you'll have the best of both worlds!

Serve and Return In serving, mix high and low serves judiciously: high if your opponent is a snail-like mover and mushy

Diagram 9: Placement of doubles serves. S: Server SP: Server's Partner R: Receiver 1 low backhand centre 2 low centre to the body 3 low forehand centre 4 drive, high or flick serve 5 flick or high serve 6 low serve to outside corner.

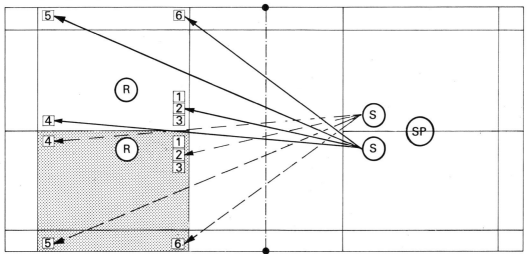

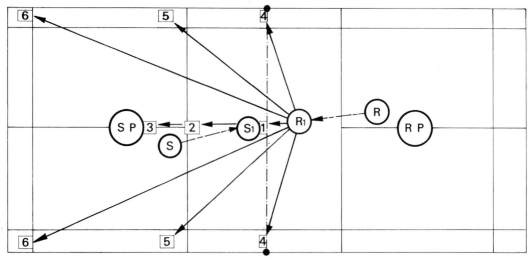

Diagram 10: Return of doubles serves. $S-S_1$: Server following in. $R-R_1$: Receiver moving in early. SP: Server's partner RP: Receiver's partner 1: net shot into body 2: brush shot 'through' advancing server 3: dab into the server's partner 4: net shots 5: half-court pushes 6 fast dabs to back corners.

Diagram 11: Men's doubles formations. A(N): Attacker near the net A(B): Attacker at the back D^1 and D^2: Defensive positions. If A(N) moves to play a lob at X he must then retreat to D^1 while his partner moves across to D^2 for a defensive, side by side formation. Meanwhile one of their opponents, D^1 moves to the shuttle to become A(B) while his partner moves quickly in to become A(N). This is an aggressive, back and front formation.

muscled; low, if he has a precociously powerful smash. As a rough rule, serve high to the corners (to prevent divisive smashing down the middle as the easy option).

In return of serve, it is, as ever, best foot forward: smash high serves unless your fearful opponents have dropped rather too far back, then play drop-shots. Return low serves with net-shots to the corners and with the occasional flat push; lift deep to the backhand unashamedly if there's a real weakness there (a habit you'll have to get rid of as you move into upper echelons where there are disconcertingly few weaknesses).

General Play Once in a rally, play drop-shots to the centre off deep lobs or clears; anything short of the back doubles service line should be smashed. A quick recovery to base between strokes is essential if the attack is to be maintained. At the net, seek to dab down returns to your shots; or play tight net-shots in preference to lobbing. In defence your two basic counters are high, deep lobs off the drop-shot and pushes off smashes.

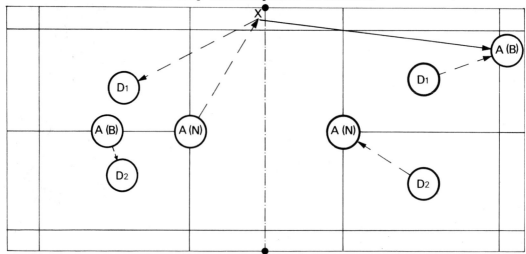

More Advanced Tactics

Positions Now that you've mastered basic positional play and your frantic elementary efforts look a little less like a tag-wrestling match, we can give a final thought to positional play. Make the best of two alternating formations.

Side by side with mid-court bases is best when you have lifted and your opponents are hitting down, so they are attacking, and you are defending. Stretch the racket to either side of you: see, you can cover the width of the court. Two long strides (all right, Samantha, three for you) and you cover any drop or clear. No real loopholes except perhaps the centre-line where you may clash rackets or each leave the shuttle for the other. Adapt your maxim now to: 'Low shots taken on the backhand; high, on the forehand'.

Back and front is best when your opponents have lifted high to you, so that you are attacking and they are defending. With your partner at the net, and so able to attack net returns, you can give your undivided attention to sustained attack from the back. No need now for you to make hurried sallies into the net from the back to reach the shuttle when it is well below tape-height and can only be lifted.

Both sides, however, are optimists – each starts back and front for service and return, each side is rightly determined to attack. For three or four shots these positions may well be maintained until one side clearly puts itself on the defensive by lifting. Whichever player is lifted to will obviously move back to deal with

Below left: A back and front (attacking) formation against side by side defence. Here Margaret Beck smashes from the back with Gillian Gilks crouched at the net to maintain the attack; their opponents are equally alert, though they have left their sidelines rather exposed in anticipation of an orthodox smash down the middle.

Below: Kevin Jolly jumps to intercept and smash a flick serve while David Eddy (Staffordshire and England) hurries in ready for any interceptions at the net.

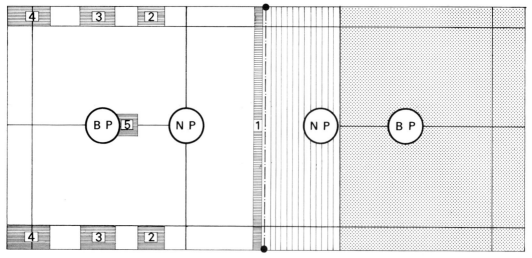

Diagram 12: Points of attack (left) and court coverage (right) for a back and front formation. BP: back partner NP: Net partner. 1 close net shots and service-returns 2 half-court pushes and fast drops 3 fast, steep smashes 4 drives 5 smashes into the body.

Court coverage for the net partner.

Court coverage for the back partner.

it; his partner will *instantly* move into position with racket up on the T-junction. So, back and front. This position they maintain as long as 'back' is hitting down even with the gentlest of drop-shots or 'front' is playing such tight upward net-shots that they cannot be hit down. So maintain attack positions as long as the opponents are lifting.

But . . . as soon as one of the attacking side lift, they obviously become defenders and adopt a 'sides' formation. The player making the lift is probably under pressure (as you say, Samantha, 'Why else would he lift?'). So it is he who moves back (or forward) into his nearest half court to defend; his less hard-pressed partner naturally moves back into the other half-court, using his eyes in the former case and his ears in the latter to help him. Positions can alter thus two or three times in a single rally.

In Return of Serve, constantly edge forward until you are aggressively, intimidatingly only a foot or so from the front service-line for male players and two or three feet for female

Watch four of the world's best men! Serving: Christian and partner Ade Chandra; Receiving: Tjun Tjun and partner Wahjudi – all Indonesians. Such is the agility and speed of Tjun Tjun that he is able to hit *down* some 85% of serves whether they are low or flick.

players. By reading your opponent's action, try to move ever earlier – and faster. Then fast pushes into the server's partner's body: pin-point it to the right side to cramp his return. Read that too, so that, with racket instantly brought up again, you can annihilate it. Vary these with pushes wide into the back corners.

If you're fractionally slow (and a fast push is risky) then try a half-court push *between* your opponents or a brush return. If slower still, an upward net-shot though now you're in the big time it will have to be camouflaged by deceptive action.

In Serving, banish the frame of mind which even toys with the thought that serving is defensive. Here, too, attack! Be confident yet careful. *Skim* the tape with a *falling* shuttle. Still serve to the centre but probe for a weakness – backhand? body? forehand? Serve *away from* the deadly *racket-head*. With a turn of the wrist occasionally find the front corners, especially the backhand one.

The flick and the drive must be concealed and given real 'zip'. Again, by probing, find where your opponent has a weakness. If nothing is working, even tempt an over-eager or weak-smashing opponent with high or very, very high serves.

Avoid error: 'See' each serve before it is hit; decide how to play it. And above all remember that the hallmark of the advanced player is the way he maintains the attack by hunting down the return. This skill is achieved only by mental, visual and physical alertness and a killer instinct. Attack!

And when your partner is serving, it is up to you by physical and mental approach to sustain the attack or to defend tenaciously. Try to take anything lifted to the backhand, round-the-head.

Attack Here once again the need is for greater accuracy, consistency and thoughtfulness of placement. Find the weakness and hammer it. Smashes should be generally straight and steep down the middle or into the inner side of the body, though occasionally vary both angle and pace. Hit drop-shots again to the middle or now temptingly nearer to the slower or more error-prone partner.

Below left: Care and concentration. Delfs prepares to ease his serve a fraction of an inch above the tape while his partner Skovgaard, defensively poised, watches the receiver's action for an early warning (a tenth of a second!) of where his attack will be launched.

Below: A well-placed drop shot to the centre seems bound to lead to a clash of rackets between Tjun Tjun (left) and Wahjudi.

Tsuchida (Japan) clips the tape with a quick backhand interception while his partner Iino (Japan) is very much on his toes – just in case!

Play as little as possible back-handed; move fractionally faster to hit round-the-head. Use too the fast, flat attacking clears as occasional shock tactics against opponents who, with touching faith in your sportsmanship, edge in too far towards the net anticipating your none too skilfully concealed drop-shot. Sustain the attack at all costs by recovering fast to hit shots down.

At the net it is the same cry – sustained attack. Try to take more, but this is worse than useless if your shots are uncontrolled and your poaching unnerves and unsights your partner. If your opponents play net-shots, move in a foot or so and then strain every sinew to take the shuttle tape-height playing tight upward net-shots or, much better, downward dabs. If they are playing half-court shots or drives, drop back a little and try to intercept with downward dabs or net-shots. Low, attacking lobs can be dealt with effectively by controlled dead-racket shots that drop the shuttle back just over the net. Stretch that arm!

Defence Here again the accent must be on a wider range of shots played *earlier*. Now your answer to the drop is not the spineless lob; see it earlier, take it earlier, and you can tumble it disconcertingly back as a net-shot. On rare days of heaven-sent speed and triumph you will even be able to dab it down!

Pushes or drives into the body you'll now nimbly side-step, returning them with interest or steering them into untenanted mid-court areas.

Even the smash, if spotted *off* the racket, can be met earlier and higher and therefore pushed flatter or even driven into the smasher's body or half-court areas. Deploy your whole range of defensive strokes. Against a flat smasher move in and chance the dab; against a sluggish one, the wrist-flick; against an unfit one, the lob. Except in the last case, follow in intelligently to maintain the attack by dabbing down any cramped returns.

You are now dealing in inches not feet, in *tenths* of seconds, not seconds. So it's a matter of practice, length, taking shots earlier,

Barbara Sutton (Staffordshire and England) plays a fast net-skimming shot to the far sideline.

placing them more exactly (and deceptively) and not making grossly careless errors. It's the low serve skimming the tape – not two inches above it; the smash into the inner side of the body, not onto the racket; the net interception off the tape, not the short lob; the ability to return the 'impossible'; the concentration, control and care that eliminates unforced errors. Those are the things that count!

For Ladies All that for you too, Samantha, but, since a woman cannot hit as hard as a man, you may clear and lob more often because not only will your opponent's return lack thunderous retribution it may even be downright weak. So use the smash less; the clear more. So too hammer the backhand more with drive serves as well as lobs. And, since interception will be slower, drop-shots may float more to give you still better length. Flicks lose their raison d'etre against comfortably-built ladies hugging the back service-line rather than the front!

Eddie Sutton uses his reach to meet the shuttle early and hit it down.

53

Chapter Eleven
Mixed Doubles

Basic Tactics

Men's and ladies' doubles are full of hard hitting; in mixed, the accent is more on subtlety, delicacy of touch, accuracy, deception, chess-like tactics and, as ever, speed of foot. A joyous game of subtle fencing.

The divorce rate among married pairs is high. The smiling 'Hard luck, dear' to the dolly-bird partner tends all too easily to become the scowling 'Why on earth . . !' to the unfortunate spouse. Still, Sam and Samantha, give it a whirl! After all it *was* 'for better, for worse'. And the Ubers *were* All-England Champions! Set your sights high!

Court coverage is simplified because the lady's domain is strictly delineated: from the net to the front service line; the man covers the rest of the court, two-thirds of it. If you played sides, Samantha, you would, on court, as you do off, attract the joyous and undivided attention of the male sex. There, at least, you just couldn't cope. But at the net you can use your quickness and touch to the full.

And let me make it clear from the outset that the male player is there, not quite solely but largely to make openings for his partner! *And* that partner has twice as difficult a task as he has. Yes, I know she covers only one-third of the court, but, at the net she has half the time to see the shuttle, and that shuttle is travelling *twice* as fast! That makes her task twice as difficult as the man's.

The Lady When serving, the lady *positions* herself three feet from the front service line and near the centre line. Receiving – as

Mixed doubles at their fastest! David Eddy smashes round-the-head to the sideline gap left by Derek Talbot. Gillian Gilks is beautifully poised for the possible cross-court alternative; Sue Whetnall with that abominable dropped racket will certainly need her super-fast reflexes.

Learn from two of the world's best mixed pairs. Mike Tredgett and Nora Perry (England) serving to Lene Koppen and Steen Skovgaard (Denmark). After reading this chapter think out for yourself the reasons for each player's position.

explained earlier. When her partner serves, the lady stands always just to the left of the T-junction and leaning to the left. When her partner is receiving she stands in her half-court as near the T-junction as she can without laying herself open to grievous bodily harm. (Never obstruct your partner or obscure your opponent's view.) Basic position: on T-junction, racket up, on balls of the feet, observant.

After serving, the lady takes up her basic position near the T-junction with racket held up. Her partner stands about six feet behind her and slightly to one side to get a better sight of the shuttle.

Why this thing of mine about T-junctions, you ask, Samantha? Because your initial position must always be as near your basic one as possible to save time and movement; and because you must always try to be as equidistant from the net-corners as possible so there is no obvious gap for your opponents to play to. Right, let's just try those out before we go any further.

Serve and Return are so important. Use the high *serve* to drive the opposing lady back, out of position; against the man, only if he is a slow mover or lacks a red-blooded smash. In *service returns*

55

go to that shuttle; meet it early – dabbing down if you can. More often than not (I hate to say it!) you'll only make impact below tape-level so then try tight upward net-shots to the corners or lobs *deep* to the *backhand*. Never, never, just poke up haplessly to centre-court for that means instant annihilation. Play net returns to the corner furthest from the incoming server.

Thinking Point : Rarely play cross-court shots until you have first moved centrally placed opponents to the side-line. Then hit flat or slightly down and use the full width *of the court.*

And in *general play*, Samantha, it's racket-up, on the toes, dabbing down anything above tape-height into the body or gaps. Avoid flat pushes to your opponent's racket or out of the back of the court. If you play from near the corner, always be alert for the cross-court reply. Second best is a tight net-shot. Under real pressure, a lift to the backhand corner is a regrettable necessity.

Thinking Point : In mixed, with the man alone covering the whole danger area, avoid lifting : Play down or flat.

One final word of warning, Samantha, never fall into temptation and try to play the shuttle once it is behind your shell-like ears. You can't control it! It's 'Eyes front!' and 'control' all the time! Don't be tempted! Don't move into your partner's domain!

The Man Remember the back two-thirds of the court is the man's domain, so you'll have to move fast. *Positions* are standard except that you stand five to six feet from the front service line to serve because, unlike in men's doubles, *you* alone must cover the back.

The lady stands always just to the left of the T-junction and leaning to the left no matter which court the man serves from.

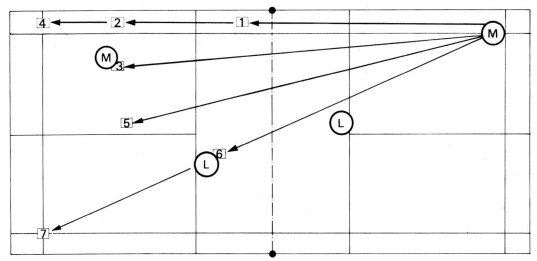

When your partner is serving or receiving and in the course of rallies you should be astride the centre-line seven to eight feet from the front service line.

Take *Serve and Return* first. These are very much as for Samantha except that in both you try to harass the opposing lady as much as you can. To hell with finer feelings – this is war! You should be rushing more low serves – especially the lady's – but be wary – for if you are drawn in and don't put the shuttle away, it will be sent smartly back over your head. Most ignominious!

Rallies tend to follow a pattern. If a serve is greeted with a flat push to the side-line, you and the opposing man will jockey for position with flat pushes just short of each other. If your opponent's push is too deep or too high, then grab the initiative and drive a straight return down the line. Better still, drive cross-court if your straight pushes have drawn both opponents to the near side-line leaving the centre clear and safe. Flat and zippy to the far side-line.

A really deep lift is hit down with a fast drop by-pass to hurry the lady or bring in the man thereby forcing a short lift. This should of course be given the full treatment: smashed *steeply* to the side-line for a winner or to make an opening for Samantha. Round-the-head strokes will be your insurance policy against a backhand corner attack. Be content just to push smashes back – away from and fast enough to pass the net-player.

Remember: don't lift; harass the possible weaker link, the lady; use the full width of the court. Oh, and Sam, don't poach; mixed doubles aren't singles you know.

More Advanced Tactics

The Lady Right, Samantha. Apprenticeship served, let's see how we can tighten up your game, turn you into a second Gillian Gilks.

The serve first. Believe it or not, if you can only develop a consistent, unassailable low serve to the T-junction that forces a lifted reply and if your return of serve is equally unassailable, strong

Diagram 13: Attack against the triangular defence. In the triangular defence the man moves to the sideline to defend against the straight smash; the lady moves nearer to the centre of the front service line of her half-court. Strokes to use against this defence are: I a deceptive drop shot 2 a smash into the gap 2 a smash into the body 4 an attacking clear to the backhand. 5 a steep smash between opponents 6 a steep smash at the lady 7 a clear to the forehand (use sparingly).

men will fight for you as partner. Develop still greater tape-skimming accuracy and consistency by endless practice, deliberation and confidence. If you're up against a 'tiger', serve a little short. And if that doesn't work then try a flick. If the opposing lady doesn't stand too far back, play flicks also for her. And as a bonus: flat, fast drives from the right court down onto her backhand. You can consign the high serve (except for a few steeplers to any lady used to playing in a low hall!) to limbo. More thought all round about exact service placement!

If the emphasis is on tight low serving it is equally on earlier, downward *returns of serve*. By practice and observation meet the shuttle within two to three feet of the tape. From there you can dab down. If the shuttle is only just above tape-height use a deceptively threatening dab turned into a gentler half-court push. This goes just 'through' the girl to drop short of the man in what, for all too obvious reasons, is known as the 'divorce area'. It brings them close together physically (but not spiritually!) and opens up acres of untenanted court.

Speed again is the answer to the flick and the high serves that have caused no little concern in your camp. Closer observation to spot the tell-tale hints of flick and instant acceleration are the essentials. Once back behind the shuttle, hit *down*. Play a smash if you can make a winner. If less sanguine, try a thoughtfully-placed, half-smash or fast drop to give you more time for instant recovery into the net.

Beware uncontrolled interception attempts while you're on the move or wild over-optimistic dabs at the net out of court. Seek to position yourself: to cover two-thirds of the net-length (the distant one-third is yours, Sam); and to place yourself within that area so you can cover both straight and cross-court net-returns.

In the rallies sternly refuse to be chicken by lifting and show a greater determination to outplay your opponent with ever tighter net-shots. Also play more well-anticipated and controlled net

Diagram 14: The lady's return of high serve and her recovery. Her possible strokes are: 1 a deceptive slow drop 2 a half or cut smash 3 a smash into the man's right side 4 an attacking clear to the backhand.

The area to be covered by the lady for her next shot. The man covers the rest of the court.

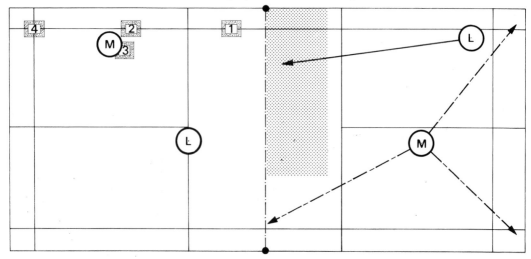

interceptions hit *steeply* to the divorce area and not flat to the
man's racket, or he will run you ragged.

Defence against the smash is always a tricky problem. There
are three possibilities. Either you can drop back to sides, as in
ladies' doubles; a ploy which won't appeal to Sam, or you, as you
will immediately become 'Target for Tonight'. Or you can cower
under the net . . . which obviously doesn't suit your 'have a go'
nature Samantha, and leaves too much for Sam to cover. Or you
can adopt the 'triangular defence' formation with Sam taking the
straight, and you, the cross-court smash. Work out the permuta-
tions and combinations in the diagram for yourself – and practise
all of them both in attack and defence.

The Man What I said to Samantha about the *serve* applies equally
to you. You can, by serving from the side line, increase the angle
of a drive serve flat into the very backhand corner. If weakly
countered, it presents points for the taking provided you've worked
out who takes what. If the side-line drive serve is effectively
counter-attacked with a round-the-head smash or Danish Wipe to
your deep backhand, forget it.

Return of serve? More half-court pushes. Even try a very
deceptive flat clear deep to your opponent's forehand (!). By
shaping to play it backhanded and to the backhand you set your
male opponent in cowardly flight; a quick turn of the wrist sends
it deceptively to the forehand. *Attack* every serve – you gain a five-
point psychological advantage.

In rallies force the pace with jump smashes, the occasional flat
attacking clear, and still more deception (not showy trick shots but
consistent deception based on 'holding' and angling the shuttle to
wrongfoot your opponent). *Perfect your backhand* so that you can
whip back smashes, play crisp drop-shots, straight and cross-
court, and smashes, even if they are pale shadows of your forehand.

When the man is returning
service his partner may stand
either behind and to his left
or in front of him and leaning
to her left. The former
position is preferred when
the lady is strong and quick,
but the latter is more common.
In both cases, the lady must
try to hit the shuttle downwards.

59

Chapter Twelve
Final Points

New Week's Resolutions

Each week find time to re-read (and re-think) the appropriate passages and practise, both in and out of a game situation, the following vital skills. Concentrate on just *one* point at a time!

1 **Grip** Practise changing from one grip to another. Check at the beginning, *in the middle*, and at the end of a rally that you are holding the racket correctly. (pp. 17–18)

2 **Backswing** Ensure your backswing is full, early and unhurried in all strokes. (p. 22)

3 **Forward Swing** Throw – don't dab – the racket-head so that at impact the arm is *straight*. (p. 23)

4 **Impact** Make sure you are hitting *into* and *through* the shuttle with racket aimed at a definite *target*. (p. 23)

5 **Recovery** Always recover your balance and return *instantly* to your base. (p. 20)

6 **Footwork** Bounce lightly, *feet never still*, between shots; strive for swifter acceleration. (pp. 20–21)

7 **Eye** Watch that shuttle from racket to racket so helping to start early and to avoid careless errors. (pp. 18–19)

8 **Wrist** Fully cock and uncock the wrist in all power strokes but don't 'snatch' at or 'snare' the shuttle. *Hear* the swish; *feel* the crack. (p. 18)

9 **Body** Swing your body into power shots; sway it into touch ones. Be body conscious! (p. 19)

10 **Brain** Use your head. Think 'placement'. Probe your opponent's weaknesses.

11 **Concentrate** Concentrate 100% on the shuttle in and between each stroke of every rally of each game.

12 **Error-free** Without being too defensive try to eliminate all unforced errors (*gift points*).

13 **Smash** Concentrate on: 1 *steepness*; 2 *placement*; and 3 *consistency* as well as power. (p. 28)

14 **Drop-shots and Clears** Check for *length* – and some deception. (pp. 25–27)

15 **Backhand** Practise at every opportunity – eliminate weakness. Hit down with smash and drop. Attack your opponents. (p. 35)

16 **Serve** Seek net-skimming *accuracy* in your low serve; kick yourself forward for short or out of court serves. Add to its effectiveness with a deceptively identical *last-second* flick. (pp. 32–33, 36)

17 **Return of Serve** By improved poise, position, push off and observation seek to meet all serves *in front of* the front service line as near the tape as possible and attack them. (pp. 33–34)

18 **Server's and Receiver's Partners** As above do everything you can to *sustain attack* or maintain a *last-ditch defence*. (p. 52)

19 **Defence** Experiment with different returns: see the shuttle as it leaves the opponent's racket. (pp. 39–40)

20 **Net** Be alert – racket up, on the balls of the feet, observant. Take only what you can *control*. (p. 56)

21 **Net-Shots** Improve upward net-shots; eschew chicken-hearted *lifts*. Ensure *dabs* are *downward* into a gap or a body, not fast and rising onto the racket. (pp. 30 and 40)

22 **Drop-Shots** Meet these at *tape-height* – not floor level. (pp. 52–53)

23 **Serve** Practise *all* the many serves; have a *reason* for playing each. Anticipate and hunt down the return.

24 **Cross-courting** Particularly in mixed, *avoid cross-courting* until you have lured opponents away from the centre. (p. 56)

Index

Acknowledgments

The author and publishers gratefully acknowledge the assistance of Gillian Gilks (England) and Pedro Blach (Spain).

The photographs were taken by the following: J. S. Birchall, Anderton 51 left; L. Eling, Basingstoke 45 left and right, 51 right; G. J. Habbin, Tadworth 44 left, 49 left, 54; Hamlyn Group Picture Library 13, 39, 52, 55 top; K. Hampshire, Ossett 9 right; R. J. Potter, Colchester 50; M. Rees, Crowborough 8; L. C. H. Ross, Totton

pages 4/5, pages 62/63, 9 left, 21 top, bottom left, bottom right, 22 top, 37 bottom right, 38 far right, 43 left and right, 53 top and bottom, 60; N. Skinner, Horsham 49 right; A. Walker 20 top.

The remaining photographs were taken for The Hamlyn Group by Don Morley – All-sport, Morden. The diagrams are by Chris Ake.